I0815642

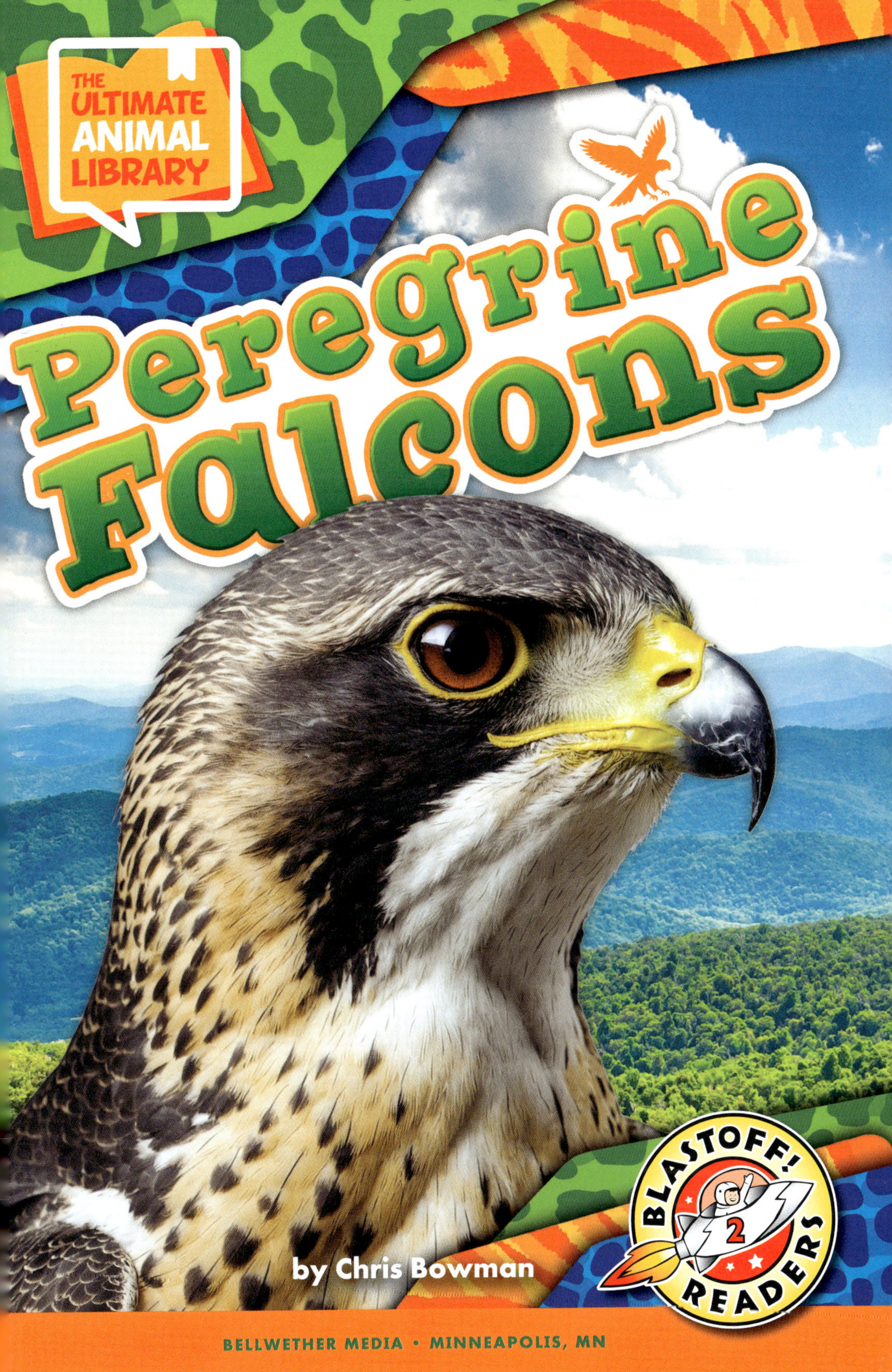
THE ULTIMATE ANIMAL LIBRARY
Peregrine Falcons
by Chris Bowman
BLASTOFF! READERS 2
BELLWETHER MEDIA • MINNEAPOLIS, MN

Blastoff! Readers are carefully developed by literacy experts to build reading stamina and move students toward fluency by combining standards-based content with developmentally appropriate text.

Level 1 provides the most support through repetition of high-frequency words, light text, predictable sentence patterns, and strong visual support.

Level 2 offers early readers a bit more challenge through varied sentences, increased text load, and text-supportive special features.

Level 3 advances early-fluent readers toward fluency through increased text load, less reliance on photos, advancing concepts, longer sentences, and more complex special features.

★ **Blastoff! Universe**

Reading Level

Grade K

Grades 1–3

Grade 4

This edition first published in 2026 by Bellwether Media, Inc.

Library of Congress Cataloging-in-Publication Data

LC record for Peregrine Falcons available at: https://lccn.loc.gov/2025003942

Editor: Elizabeth Neuenfeldt   Series Designer: Veah Demmin

Printed in the United States of America, North Mankato, MN.

Table of Contents

What Are Peregrine Falcons?

Peregrine falcons are large **raptors**. They live on most **continents**. These birds are known for their speed. They are the fastest animals in the world!

Peregrine Falcon Report

Range

range =

Status in the Wild

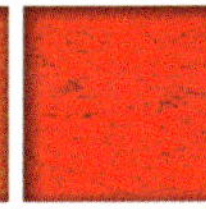

least concern

Habitats

coastlines

deserts

forests

mountains

These falcons have mostly dark gray or blue feathers. White feathers cover their necks.

Their bellies are white
with black or brown spots.

Peregrine falcons have good eyesight. They can see **prey** from far away.

Their sharp beaks take down prey.

Peregrine falcons have large, pointed wings. They have long tails.

These birds have big **talons**. Their talons are very sharp.

Spot a Peregrine Falcon

large, pointed wings

long tail

big, sharp talons

Fast Flyers

Peregrine falcons often live near **coastlines**. They often stay on **cliffs**.

Many call forests or mountains home. Some even live in **deserts**.

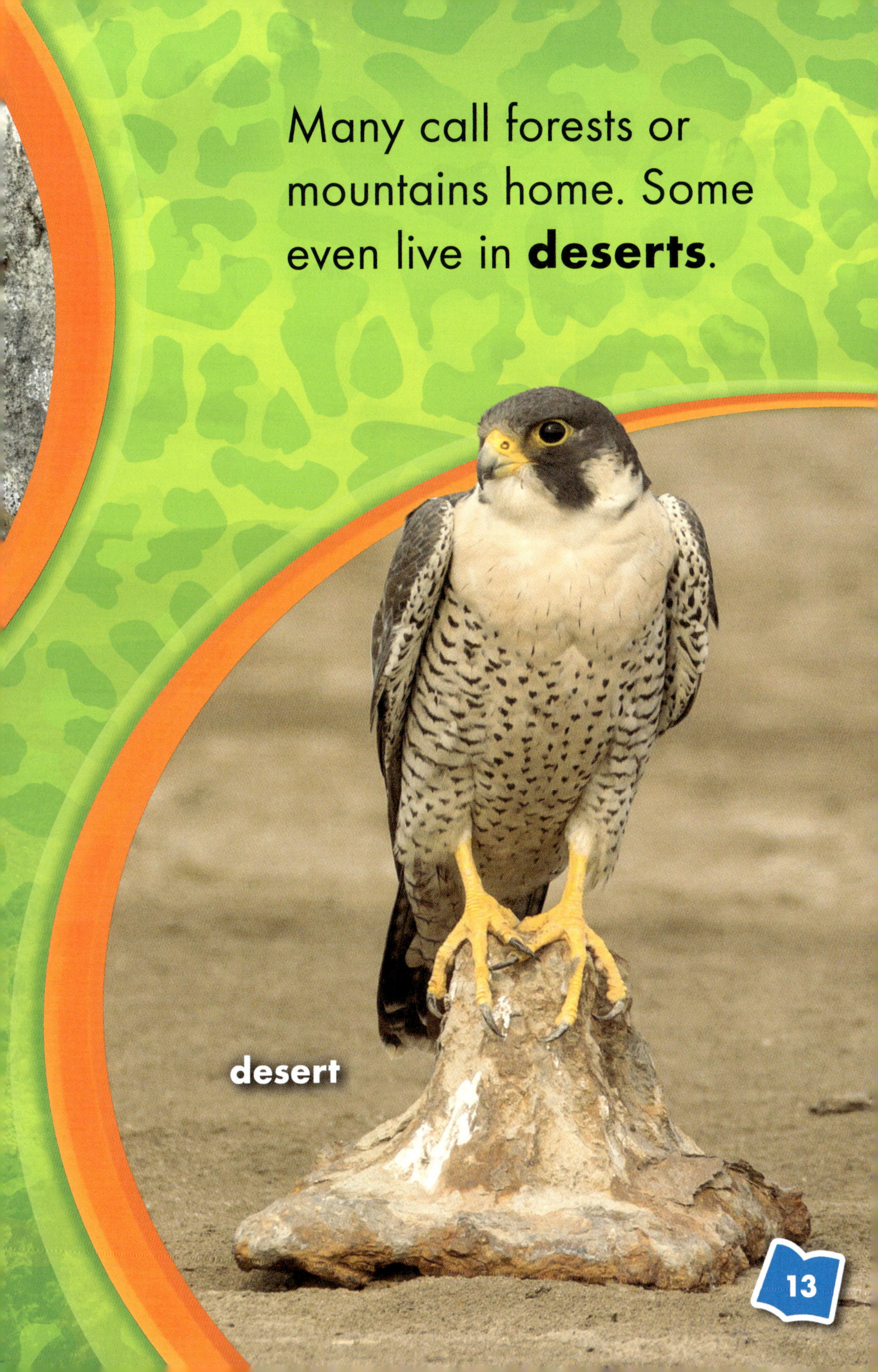

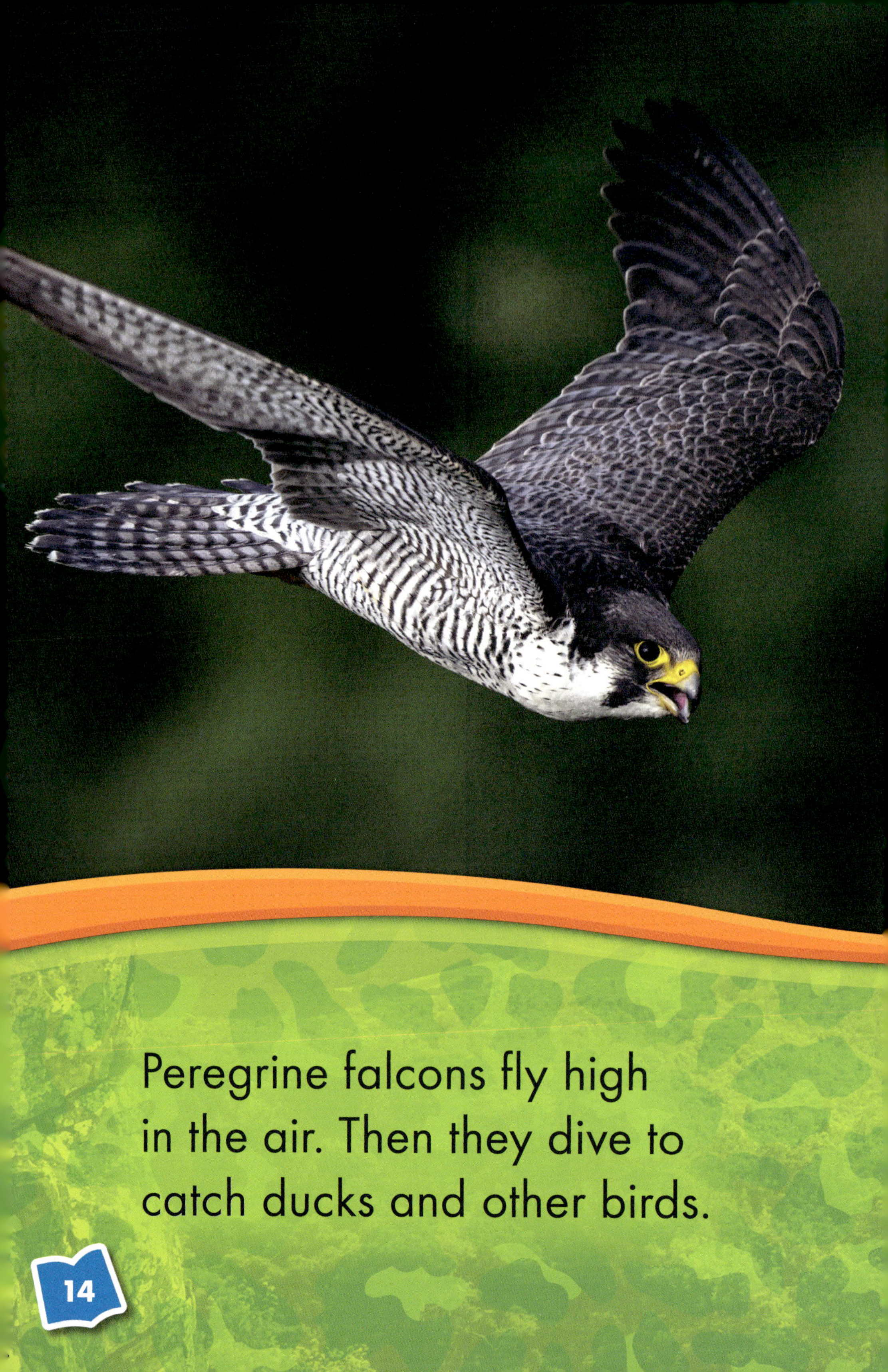

Peregrine falcons fly high in the air. Then they dive to catch ducks and other birds.

They can dive up to 200 miles (322 kilometers) per hour!

Peregrine falcons try to speed away from **predators**.

gyrfalcon

Eagles and great horned owls hunt them. Gyrfalcons hunt them, too.

Growing Up

Female peregrines lay up to five eggs at a time. The eggs **hatch** about a month later.

Eyases come out. They can fly about six weeks later. They are now **fledglings**.

eyas

eggs

Fledglings may stay with their parents for several more weeks. They learn how to hunt.

Then it is time to find food!

Life of a Peregrine Falcon

Name of Babies

eyases

Number of Eggs

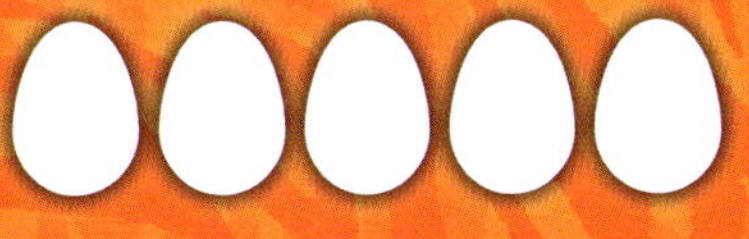

up to 5

Time Spent with Parents

at least 6 weeks

Life Span

around 19 years

Glossary

cliffs—high, steep surfaces of rock, earth, or ice

coastlines—areas where lands meet large bodies of water

continents—large areas of land

deserts—dry lands with few plants and little rainfall

eyases—baby peregrine falcons

fledglings—young birds that have feathers for flight

hatch—to break open

predators—animals that hunt other animals for food

prey—animals that are hunted by other animals for food

raptors—large birds that hunt other animals; raptors have excellent eyesight and powerful talons.

talons—the strong, sharp claws of peregrine falcons and other raptors

To Learn More

AT THE LIBRARY

Jaycox, Jaclyn. *Falcons*. North Mankato, Minn.: Pebble, 2023.

Kenney, Karen Latchana. *Harpy Eagles*. Minneapolis, Minn.: Bellwether Media, 2021.

Scheffer, Janie. *Bald Eagles*. Minneapolis, Minn.: Bellwether Media, 2025.

ON THE WEB

FACTSURFER

Factsurfer.com gives you a safe, fun way to find more information.

1. Go to www.factsurfer.com.

2. Enter "peregrine falcons" into the search box and click 🔍.

3. Select your book cover to see a list of related content.

Index

The images in this book are reproduced through the courtesy of: Malikbros, cover (peregrine falcon); Jon Bilous, cover background, interior background; arifafrin, cover (peregrine falcon icon); JT Jeeraphun, p. 3; Harry Collins, pp. 4, 7, 10, 11; mifurman, p. 6; Jeff_DuBay, p. 9; Ken Griffiths, pp. 10-11, 12, 18-19; manjeet & yograj jadeja/ Alamy, p. 13; kojihirano, pp. 14-15; Tomas Hulik, p. 15 (eagles); Arnau, p. 15 (peregrine falcon); FotoRequest, p. 15 (blue jays); clsdesign, p. 15 (ducks); Ron Scott/ Wirestock Creators, p. 15 (gryfalcons); Chris Hill, p. 15 (owls); Chrisoph Bosch/ Alamy, p. 16; Rob Palmer Photography, p. 17; Alexander Erdbeer, pp. 18, 21; Howard Freshman, p. 20; Jrs, p. 23.